Understanding LOCAL MAPS

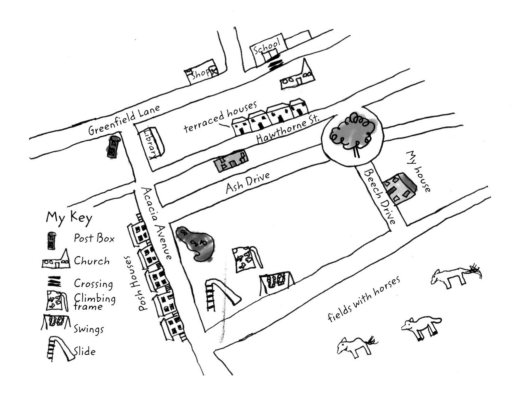

Jack and Meg Gillett

Published in paperback in 2014 by Wayland
Copyright © Wayland 2014

Wayland
338 Euston Road
London NW1 3BH

Wayland Australia
Hachette Children's Books
Level 17/207 Kent Street
Sydney, NSW 2000

Managing Editor: Rasha Elsaeed
Editor: Katie Dicker
Picture researcher: Shelley Noronha
Designer: Alix Wood. Illustrator: Catherine Ward
Author dedication: 'For Sue and Alan'

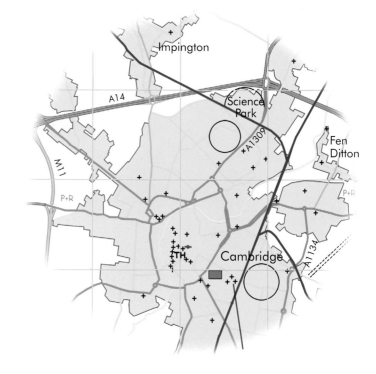

Picture Credits
Front cover, top left: skyscan/©Blom Aerofilms. Page 4, Figure A, left: © skyscan. Page 4, Figure A, right: Getmapping. Page 5, Figure B: Daily Information/www.dailyinfo.co.uk. Page 6, middle and bottom right: Jack & Meg Gillett. Page 7, Figure A: Reproduced by permission of Geographer's A–Z Map Co. Licence No: B4394 © Crown Copyright 2008. All rights reserved. Licence number 100017302. Page 10, Figure A: Maps International. Page 12, bottom left: © Patrice Thomas/Hemis/Corbis. Page 15, Figure B; Page 23, bottom; Page 27, Figure D: Reproduced by permission of Ordnance Survey on behalf of HMSO. © Crown copyright 2008. All rights reserved. Ordnance Survey Licence number 100047991. Page 21, Figure B, top left: © Roy Rainford/Robert Harding World Imagery/Corbis. Page 21, Figure B, middle left: © skyscan/R West. Page 21, Figure B, bottom left: © Ashley Cooper/Corbis. Page 21, Figure B, top right: © Mike McQueen/Corbis. Page 21, Figure B, middle right: © skyscan/B Evans. Page 21, Figure B, bottom right: © Andrew Brown; Ecoscene/Corbis. Page 22: Chris McHugh/Rex Features. Page 23, top left: skyscan/©Blom Aerofilms. Page 24, middle right: Jack & Meg Gillett. Page 25, Figure C: Based on OS Landranger 154. Page 26, Figure A, B & C: Alan & Sue Colgate.

Page 30 may be reproduced for class use solely within the purchaser's school or college.

Note to parents and teachers: Every effort has been made by the publishers to ensure that websites referred to in the book are suitable for children. However, because of the nature of the Internet, it is impossible to guarantee that the contents of these sites will not be altered. We strongly advise that Internet access is supervised by a responsible adult.

British Library Cataloguing in Publication Data
Gillett, Jack
   Understanding local maps. – (Maps and mapping skills)
   1. Map reading – Juvenile literature 2. Map drawing – Juvenile literature
   I. Title II. Gillett, Meg
   912'.014

ISBN 978 0 7502 8474 5
Printed in China
10 9 8 7 6 5 4 3

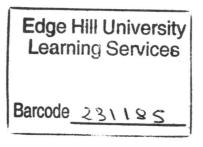
Wayland is a division of Hachette Children's Books, an Hachette UK Company
www.hachette.co.uk

Contents

A bird's eye view

Aerial photographs help **cartographers** to draw accurate maps of a local area, because they show the Earth's surface from a **bird's eye view**. Aerial photographs can be oblique (taken from above, and at an angle) or vertical (taken looking straight down).

The photographs in Figure A show a view of central Oxford, comparing the two types of aerial photograph. Map-makers prefer to use vertical photographs rather than oblique photographs. This is because maps are always drawn as vertical, bird's eye views. Vertical images also help map-makers to work out the measurements and **directions** between landscape **features**, such as schools and libraries, or the routes of different roads.

Map details

Figure B shows a map of central Oxford. You can see that map-makers leave out small details, such as the way a building looks. Instead, they draw lines and boxes to show its shape and size.

▲ These aerial photographs are oblique (left) and vertical (right) views. They show the same area of central Oxford in different types of detail.

You can also see in Figure B that maps include information you can't see from the air – street names and the uses of particular buildings, such as Oxford's many famous university colleges.

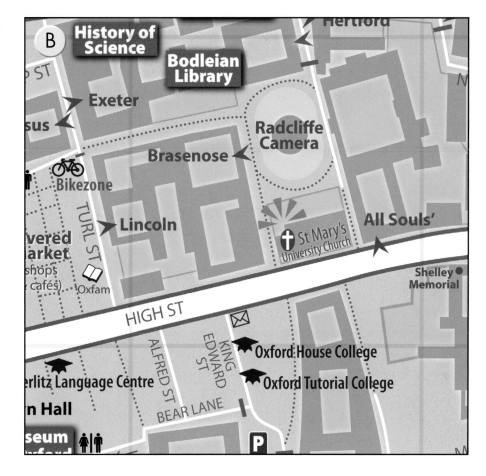

▲ *This map of central Oxford shows the same area as the photographs in Figure A. Maps provide us with more detailed information than aerial photographs.*

Do it yourself

1 Look at the images in Figure A and Figure B. List one feature which:
 a you can see on the oblique photograph but not on the vertical photograph.
 b is shown on the map but not on the two photographs.
 c is in the photographs but not on the map.

2 Using the website **http://www1.getmapping.com** type in your postcode (or town name) to view a vertical image and a map of your local area. You can interact with the image on-screen to view the area at different scales. Or, you might like to use the Google homepage (**www.google.co.uk**) by clicking on maps, then typing in your chosen place name or postcode.

Using co-ordinates

Street maps use grids of horizontal and vertical lines to help visitors find their way around a town. Each map square is given a code with a letter, followed by a number. We call these **co-ordinates**. The letters are printed below the map and the numbers go up the side.

The map in Figure A shows a grid system for the centre of Huddersfield, a large town in West Yorkshire. Two examples of number-letter codes for this map are:
- The square in the top, right-hand corner of the map is **D6**.
- **C1** gives you the third square along the bottom row of the map.

If you have played the game 'Battleships', you will be familiar with this grid system!

▲ *These children are playing 'Battleships'. They are using co-ordinates to find square G5.*

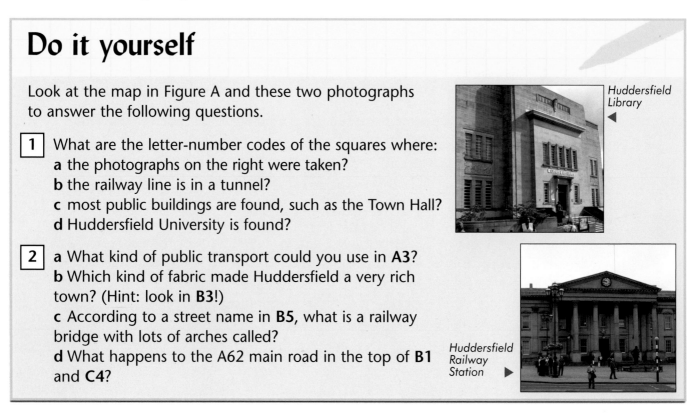

Do it yourself

Look at the map in Figure A and these two photographs to answer the following questions.

Huddersfield Library ◄

1   What are the letter-number codes of the squares where:
    a the photographs on the right were taken?
    b the railway line is in a tunnel?
    c most public buildings are found, such as the Town Hall?
    d Huddersfield University is found?

2   **a** What kind of public transport could you use in **A3**?
    b Which kind of fabric made Huddersfield a very rich town? (Hint: look in **B3**!)
    c According to a street name in **B5**, what is a railway bridge with lots of arches called?
    d What happens to the A62 main road in the top of **B1** and **C4**?

Huddersfield Railway Station ►

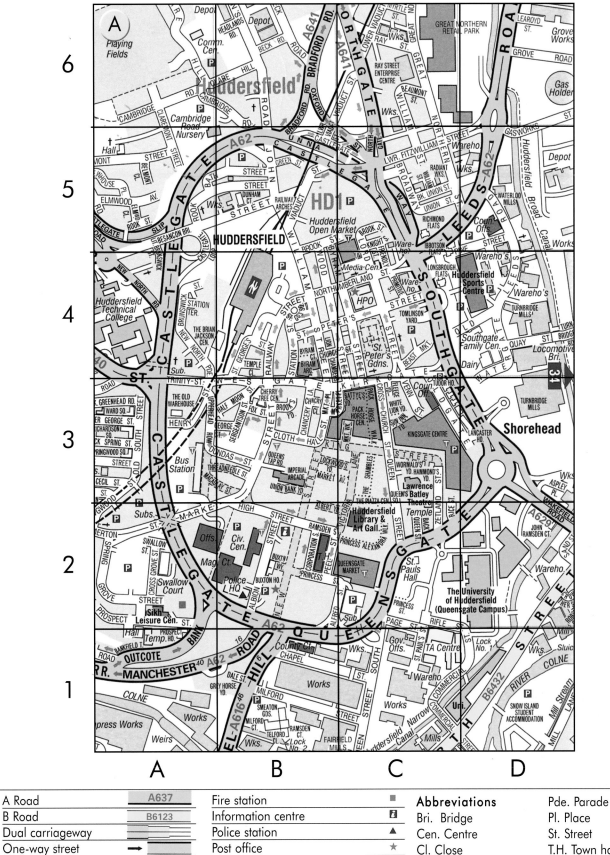

A Road	A637
B Road	B6123
Dual carriageway	
One-way street	→
Pedestrianised road	
Railway	Station / Heritage Station / Level Crossing / Tunnel
Built-up area	CHURCH / STREET
Car park	P
Church or chapel	†

Fire station	■
Information centre	i
Police station	▲
Post office	★
Toilet	▽
Educational establishment	
Industrial building	
Public building	
Shopping centre or market	

Abbreviations

Bri. Bridge	Pde. Parade
Cen. Centre	Pl. Place
Cl. Close	St. Street
Ct. Court	T.H. Town hall
Gdns. Gardens	Offs. Offices
Gth. Garth	Temp. Temple
Ho. House	HPO. Head post office
Lib. Library	Wks. Works
	Wy. Way

Drawing maps from memory

Sometimes, we memorise what places look like in the form of a **mental map**. These maps are incredibly useful because they remind us how to get to our destination and what we might see along the route. Our memories of regular journeys become increasingly reliable over time.

The map in Figure A shows the school route taken by Jordan Smith, who lives at number 3, Beech Drive. It shows the roads he has to walk along, as well as some familiar landmarks (features) on the way, such as the beech tree which gave his street its name! The library reminds him to turn right onto Greenfield Lane.

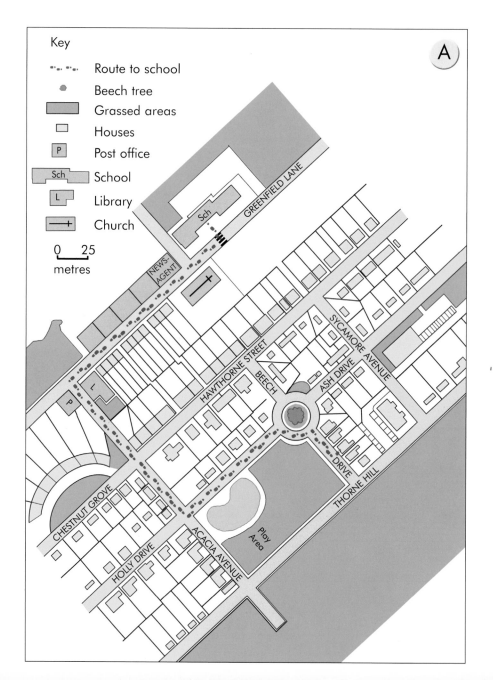

Key

- Route to school
- Beech tree
- Grassed areas
- Houses
- P Post office
- Sch School
- L Library
- Church

0   25
metres

This is an accurate map of Jordan's route from home to school. The map has been carefully drawn to scale. ▶

(B)

▲ Jordan's mental map.

My Key
- Post Box
- Church
- Crossing
- Climbing frame
- Swings
- Slide

Map labels: Greenfield Lane, terraced houses, Shop, School, Library, Hawthorne St., Acacia Avenue, Ash Drive, Beech Drive, My house, Posh Houses, fields with horses

The map in Figure B is of the same area. It has the same roads, but the landmarks look different because this is Jordan's mental map of his route to school. Jordan's mental map is not drawn to **scale**. It shows what Jordan imagines the roads look like from a bird's eye view. However, he has drawn some landmarks from a ground-level view, to make it easier to understand!

Do it yourself

1. Choose a short route that you know well. It could be your walk to school, to a friend's house or to a local shop.

2. Draw your own mental map of the route you have chosen. Your map must show the roads you walk along and any important landmarks on the way. Label them all – just like Jordan did. You might want to do this 'in rough' first!

3. Now ask a school friend or a family member to say how accurate your map looks. Ask them to suggest any other landmarks that you could have added.

Tourist maps

People often buy and use maps when they visit a new place that is unfamiliar to them. Some map-making companies produce maps designed for people on a day-trip or a holiday. These maps are drawn to highlight tourist attractions, including local markets, restaurants and theatres.

Figure A shows a tourist map of central London. These maps are called **thematic maps** – they focus on one theme – in this case, tourism. The maps often have a key to show different types of attractions, as well as the names of some of the most famous ones (Figure B).

B **LONDON'S Top Ten attractions**

1. British Museum
2. Buckingham Palace
3. Houses of Parliament
4. London Eye
5. Tower of London
6. St Paul's Cathedral
7. Trafalgar Square
8. Tower Bridge
9. River Thames river cruises
10. HMS Belfast

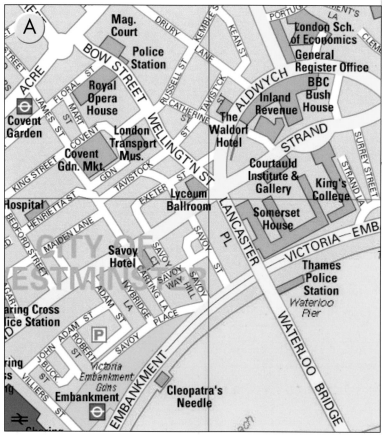

Other tourist maps are designed to help people explore an area, perhaps recommending a walking trail that passes interesting sites. Figure C shows an extract from such a map.

◄ *This tourist map of central London shows the location of some key attractions, such as art galleries and museums.*

10

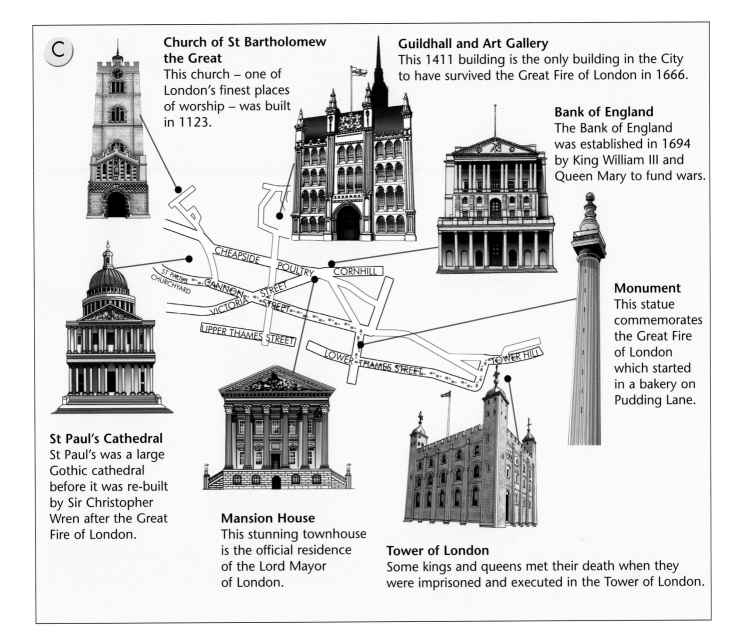

C

Church of St Bartholomew the Great
This church – one of London's finest places of worship – was built in 1123.

Guildhall and Art Gallery
This 1411 building is the only building in the City to have survived the Great Fire of London in 1666.

Bank of England
The Bank of England was established in 1694 by King William III and Queen Mary to fund wars.

CHEAPSIDE

POULTRY

CORNHILL

ST PAULS CHURCHYARD

CANNON STREET

VICTORIA STREET

UPPER THAMES STREET

LOWER THAMES STREET

TOWER HILL

Monument
This statue commemorates the Great Fire of London which started in a bakery on Pudding Lane.

St Paul's Cathedral
St Paul's was a large Gothic cathedral before it was re-built by Sir Christopher Wren after the Great Fire of London.

Mansion House
This stunning townhouse is the official residence of the Lord Mayor of London.

Tower of London
Some kings and queens met their death when they were imprisoned and executed in the Tower of London.

▲ *This extract from a walking tour of historic London shows pictures and information about some of the city's oldest buildings.*

Do it yourself

1 Copy a street map of the area in which you live or in which you go to school. Choose about six places in your chosen area that you like or are important to you. Take photographs of them, and write a sentence or two about each one. Now plan a walk around the area that passes each place in turn. Mark this route on your map and arrange the photographs and their descriptions around the edge to provide your family and friends with a really enjoyable tour!

Maps at sea

Most of the maps we come across show places on land – but what about the seas and oceans? Ferries sail constantly between ports to transport people and goods from place to place. Sailors need to know which route to take for the quickest and safest journey.

The shape of the seabed alters over time, in the same way that landscapes change because of erosion. The underwater landscape includes many shallow banks and deep trenches. People who work at sea need to know how deep the water is wherever they are. The map on page 13 shows how the depth of the sea changes between Britain and mainland Europe.

▲ *The busiest part of the North Sea is in the south, where it meets the English Channel. This ferry is taking passengers between Dover and Calais.*

Do it yourself

1. Use the map on page 13 to discover whether these statements about the North Sea are true or false.
   a Its central area, the Dogger Bank, is the deepest part of the North sea.
   b Its deepest part is along the coast of Norway.
   c Most of its oil fields are in the northern part.
   d Most of its gas fields are in the southern part.

2. Draw a copy of the table below and add the 'un-jumbled' names of the ferry ports written beside it. Do this using the map on page 13, and an atlas map of the North Sea.

Countries		Ferry ports
	Belgium	
	Denmark	
	England	
	France	
	Germany	
	Netherlands	
	Norway	
	Scotland	

Breneg
Chiwarh
Darenebe
Gezubreeg
Grumbah
Jesgreb
Kruknid
Luhl
Madtotrer
Rodev
Satnavreg
Slewcanet

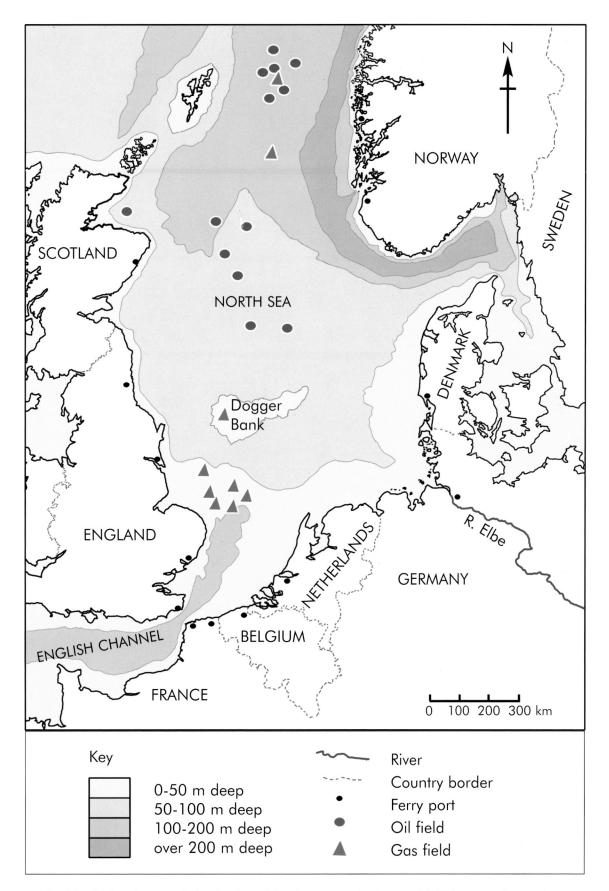

N

NORWAY

SWEDEN

SCOTLAND

NORTH SEA

Dogger
Bank

DENMARK

R. Elbe

ENGLAND

NETHERLANDS

GERMANY

BELGIUM

ENGLISH CHANNEL

FRANCE

0 100 200 300 km

Key

0-50 m deep
50-100 m deep
100-200 m deep
over 200 m deep

River
Country border
● Ferry port
● Oil field
▲ Gas field

▲ *The North Sea is one of the busiest shipping areas in the world. This map shows the location of the main ferry ports, the oil and gas fields and the depth of the water.*

Introducing O.S. maps

Ordnance Survey (O.S.) maps are a series of detailed, local maps produced for the whole of Britain. They are **topographical maps** – they show natural features (such as hills and rivers) as well as human features (such as roads and buildings).

On the following pages you will gain the skills you need to use O.S. maps, and you will become familiar with their **symbols**. These symbols are shown in the key at the back of this book. But first, look at how you can use four-figure **grid references** to locate areas on a map (Figure A).

Do it yourself

Use Figure B (and its key at the back of this book) to answer the following questions.

1. Which grid squares show:
   a Junction 14 of the M74?
   b Most of the buildings in Abington village?
   c Clydeside Farm, on the A73?
   d Castle Hill (between Abington and Crawford villages)?

2. Name the hills in these grid squares:
   a 9024   b 9228   c 9624   d 9720

3. List the meaning of seven different kinds of O.S. symbols in square 9320.

A How to give the four-figure grid reference of a location on a map

1 First write down the number of the line down the left side.

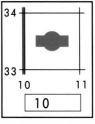

2 Now add the number of the line along the bottom. The four-figure grid reference is **10 33**.

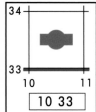

How to use a four-figure grid reference to find a location on a map

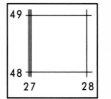

1 To find grid square 27 48, look at the vertical line numbered 27. The square you need is to the right of this line.

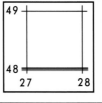

2 Find the horizontal line numbered 48. The square you need is above this line.

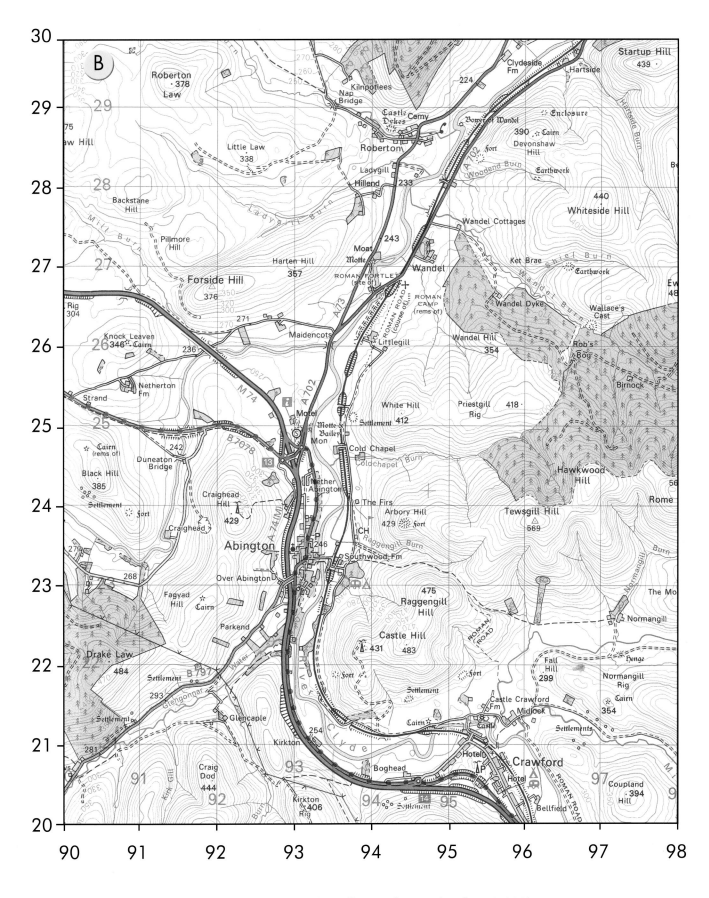

▲ *An O.S. map of part of the Upper Clyde Valley (with a scale of 1:50,000).*

Distance, direction and scale

O.S. maps can be used to work out how far any two places are apart, and discover how long it would take to travel between them. Without O.S. maps it would be hard to get to places on time! But to do this we need to understand how these maps use distance, direction and scale.

Distance and direction

Figure A shows a compass rose which has eight directions, and a line scale showing the distances on a map. Remember that directions are very easy to see on O.S. maps because North is always at the top, up the vertical grid lines.

Scale

O.S. maps like the one on page 15 have a ratio scale of 1:50,000. This means that 1 cm represents 50,000 cm (500 m) in real-life. Other maps use a line scale to show the real distance (see Figures A and B).

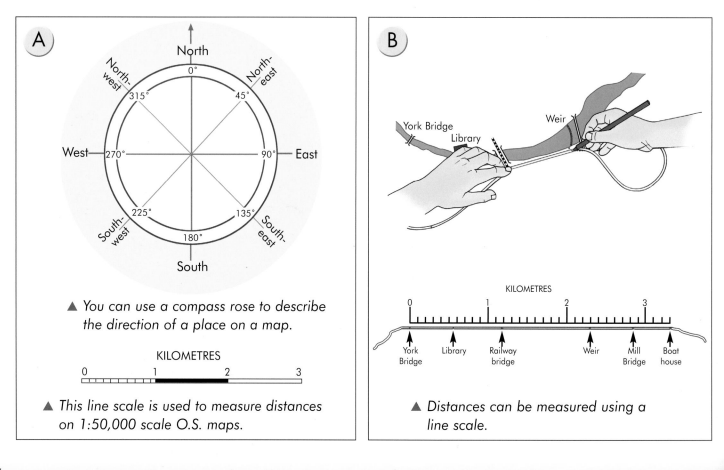

▲ You can use a compass rose to describe the direction of a place on a map.

▲ This line scale is used to measure distances on 1:50,000 scale O.S. maps.

▲ Distances can be measured using a line scale.

Six-figure grid references

Although four-figure grid references are good for locating areas on an O.S. map, they don't pinpoint the **location** of small features. This is why we prefer to use six-figure grid references. Figure C shows you how to do this.

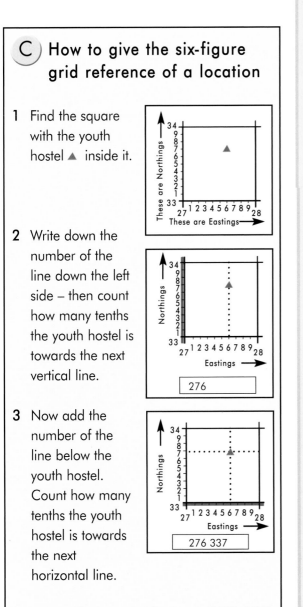

C How to give the six-figure grid reference of a location

1 Find the square with the youth hostel ▲ inside it.

2 Write down the number of the line down the left side – then count how many tenths the youth hostel is towards the next vertical line.

276

3 Now add the number of the line below the youth hostel. Count how many tenths the youth hostel is towards the next horizontal line.

276 337

4 The six-figure grid reference is **276 337**.

Do it yourself

1 Imagine that you're travelling up the M74 motorway, on your way to stay at Clydeside Farm, in southern Scotland. Using the map on page 15 and a copy of the text below, fill in all the blank spaces. To help you, there are three choices given for each curved distance!

You join the map at 958 200, due ..... of Crawford village. At Junction 14, the car is travelling due .... At 935 206, it is pointing ..... - ..... , and at 929 220, it is travelling due .... The distance it has travelled between 958 200 and 929 220 is ..... (3.2, 4.2 or 5.2) km. The direct distance between these two places is ..... km. The car has another ..... (2.0, 2.5 or 3.0) km to go before leaving the M74 at Junction 13 (at 931 245). From the roundabout near to the motorway service area, it has to go another ..... (5.9, 6.9 or 7.9) km along the A702 then the A73 before reaching Clydeside Farm. This farm is on the ..... side of the A73.

Contour lines

Map-makers have always had a problem – how do you draw maps on a flat piece of paper when the Earth's surface is bumpy? Over the centuries, cartographers have tried lots of different ways to solve this problem. Some of these are shown in Figure A.

Most of the maps in Figure A show the location of high land, but none of them tell us its exact height. Also, these early maps didn't have enough space to add important features, such as buildings and roads. Today, the most effective way to show **relief** (the height of land) is to use **contour** lines. A contour is a line joining places with exactly the same height above sea level. You can see lots of contour lines on the O.S. map on page 15, for example. This area has lots of hills of different shapes and sizes – and steep slopes because the contour lines are drawn close together.

A   **Examples of the way that early cartographers used maps to show the height of land**

Simple picture symbols

One of the earliest ways of showing hills and mountains was simply to draw a small picture of a hill.

Hachuring

Hachure lines show the direction of the slope of the land; where it is steepest they are drawn very close together.

Detailed picture symbols

Later, more detailed 'pictures' of upland features were drawn on maps; this made it hard to show any other information, such as roads and towns, on the same map!

Colour shading

This method makes it easy to see where highland and lowland areas are. A key may be used, and additional information can also be printed over the shading.

Drawing contour lines

Cartographers plot the height of the land as a series of dots across a map. They then 'join-the-dots', just like a puzzle, to produce a series of contour lines. Some of these lines are labelled with their height in metres. Contours tell us the exact height of the land, but their patterns also show how steep the land is (Figure B). Steep land has its contour lines close together, but flatter land has contour lines that are much further apart.

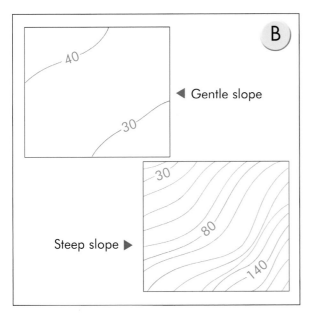

B

40

30

◀ Gentle slope

Steep slope ▶

30

80

140

▲ *These contour lines have been drawn to show a steep slope and a gentle slope.*

Another common way of showing height can be seen on the map on page 15. These are **spot heights** – small dots with numbers written next to them. You can see one, which is 378 metres above sea level, at 915 293.

Do it yourself

Make your own contoured hill and map. Follow the instructions below to make a matching hill and map.

You will need:

- plasticine or clay
- thick paper or card
- a card marked at 1 cm intervals
- a cocktail stick
- a clear plastic box
- a piece of stiff acetate (or clear plastic sheet/box lid)
- a felt-tip pen

1 Use the plasticine or clay to make a hill with a valley in it.

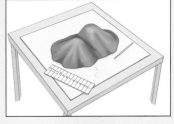

2 Take the card marked at 1 cm intervals and hold it upright. Using your cocktail stick, follow round the hill and mark off a line exactly 1 cm above the level of the table. Do the same for 2 cm, then 3 cm, etc. until you reach the top of the hill.

3 Now you have a hill with contours marked at 1 cm intervals. To draw a map, put your contoured hill into a clear plastic box. Use a piece of stiff acetate (or clear plastic) as a lid. Looking directly down, draw the contour lines on the lid with a felt-tip pen.

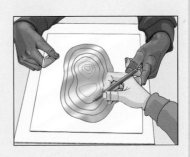

Contour patterns

Contour lines show us the height of the land and the steepness of a hill's slopes. But the patterns they create can also tell us about the shape of a landscape. Just by looking at a map, we can begin to imagine what an area looks like.

Slopes and gradients

Geographers use the word **gradient** to describe how steep a slope is. Figure A shows that steep gradients are hard to climb, whilst gentle gradients are easier to walk or cycle on. Some mountain slopes are so steep that they are almost vertical! This makes it impossible to draw separate contour lines – instead we use the symbol for cliffs (see the first contour map in Figure A). Where the land is very flat, there are no contours at all, but we can still use spot heights to give an idea of the height of the land.

Contour patterns

Groups of contour lines also tell us about the shape of the land. For example, they show where mountains, hills and valleys are located. Each landscape feature has its own special contour pattern. Figure B shows photographs of six common landscape features and a typical contour pattern to illustrate each one.

▼ *These contour lines show land that is 1) steep, 2) gently sloping and 3) flat. The children are learning which contours are easiest to walk and cycle on!*

▲ These photographs and contour patterns show six common landscape features.

Do it yourself

Which of the landscape features shown in Figure B fits each of these descriptions?

| 1 | A long, narrow area of high land (ridge). |

| 2 | A long, narrow area of lowland which is often steep on both sides; it usually has a river flowing through it (valley). |

| 3 | A mountain that has a large, flat top (plateau or flat-topped mountain). |

| 4 | Land that is so high that the contours are very close together, showing that all its sides have steep gradients ((mountain or hill). |

| 5 | This feature is gently sloping, not very high, and is surrounded by lower land (knoll). |

| 6 | Some of this land is so steep that it is almost vertical – a special symbol is used there instead of contour lines (cliff). |

The human landscape

Often, the most obvious features on O.S. maps are part of the **human landscape**. The buildings and roads that people have built tell us a lot about a place. O.S. maps also help us to see the size and shape of **settlements**.

Look at the map on page 23 – Cambridge stands out as the largest place on the map, but Girton and Milton are villages. Girton has a linear (long, narrow) shape, whilst Milton is nucleated (more rounded). Main roads such as the A1307 also stand out. They link settlements, often going right into their centres. Cambridge is a medieval city, and the streets in its **Central Business District (C.B.D.)** are too narrow for modern traffic. The city now has a **ring road** (1 km from the Town Hall) and a **by-pass** (the A14) to keep passing traffic away from its centre.

Minor roads often create distinct street patterns. For example, rows of straight, parallel roads like those in square 4657 show old, terraced houses, whereas areas of newer housing (around 460 610) have curved patterns and are further away from the C.B.D..

Useful locations

You can tell that Cambridge's C.B.D. is in square 4558 because the town hall, the bus station and several places of worship are located there. More recent developments, such as the railway station (462 572) and sports facilities (460 580) are outside the centre. Even newer developments are found at the edge of the city, such as the Science Park in square 4661. This is an ideal industrial site because it has easy access to the A10, the A14 and the A1309 and is only 5 km from the M11.

The streets are very narrow in the historic centre of Cambridge. ▶

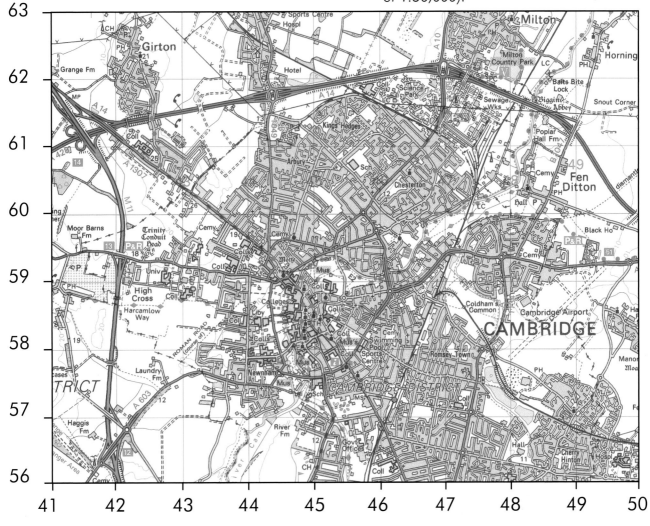

Do it yourself

1. On a map of your local area, identify at least five different human landscape features, similar to those described for Cambridge. Take photographs of these features and make a display that links the photographs with their locations on the map.

▲ *Cambridge Science Park has been built with easy access to nearby roads.*

▼ *An O.S. map of Cambridge (with a scale of 1:50,000).*

Using sketches

Geographers often use **field sketches** of the landscape to show information that is not shown on maps. Sketches are more useful than maps – and even photographs – because they allow geographers to add labels that provide extra useful information.

Look at the photograph in Figure A. This shows a row of cottages in the village of Rastrick. You can see exactly what the cottages look like in real-life. The illustration in Figure B is a field sketch of the same view. It is a realistic drawing of the photograph. There is also room around the sketch to add labels to describe the cottages in more detail.

Do it yourself

▲ *This is a field sketch of the photograph in Figure A.*

1. Draw a rough copy of Figure B.

2. Using the photograph above, add detailed labels to your sketch that give as much information as possible about the row of cottages, but not the car parked outside (because we don't put moving things on maps or field sketches). One label to start you off is 'Paved area for off-road parking'.

3. Make a field sketch of a street near to your home or school, and add as many detailed labels to it as you can.

Sketching from O.S. maps

Geographers use O.S. maps to increase their understanding of the landscape. To do this, they often make **sketch maps** like the one shown in Figure C. They use sketch maps to highlight the most important features of an area. In Figure C, labels have been added to the sketch map to summarise the map of Cambridge shown on page 23. Many people find sketch maps like this easier to understand than long, written descriptions! Which do you find easier to understand?

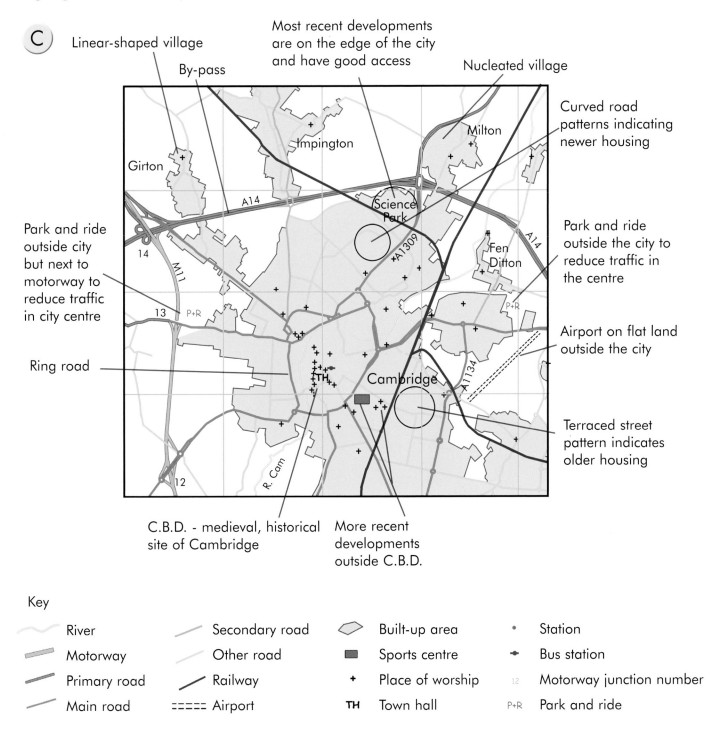

▲ A sketch map of the O.S. map shown on page 23, highlighting the human features of the Cambridge area.

Use your skills: Map practise

You have learnt lots of new map skills in this book. Now is the time to check that you really know how to use them! Use the photographs and the map in Figures A to D to see how skilful you are. You can find the answers on page 32 if you are really stuck!

1 a What do the photographs in Figures A, B and C show? Look for them in grid squares 3670, 3564 and 3864.
   b What is the six-figure grid reference of each feature?

2 Look at the map shown in Figure D.
   a What are the distances between Ramsgate and Broadstairs railway stations at 373 658 and 391 680:
      - in a straight line?
      - along the railway line between them?
   b What is the compass direction of Broadstairs' railway station from Ramsgate's station?

3 a Why could golfers in square 3970 have problems getting back to their clubhouse?
   b Using the symbols shown on the map (and the key at the back of this book), make a list of enjoyable activities people could do in their spare time south of grid line 67.
   c How are the street patterns around 383 693 and 390 705 different? Which of these housing areas is likely to have been built first?
   d Square 3967 locates the C.B.D. of Broadstairs. List the meanings of the O.S. symbols in and near to this square which tell you that the town centre is there.
   e Does the village of Manston, in square 3466, have a linear or a nucleated shape? How can you tell which one it is?

4 The Patel family are staying with friends at Bush Farm, on the edge of Manston village. They want to visit Westwood Cross Shopping Centre at 364 679. Draw a fully-labelled sketch map which shows them exactly how to get there. Your route should use the B2050 secondary road and include information about what they will see on the way.

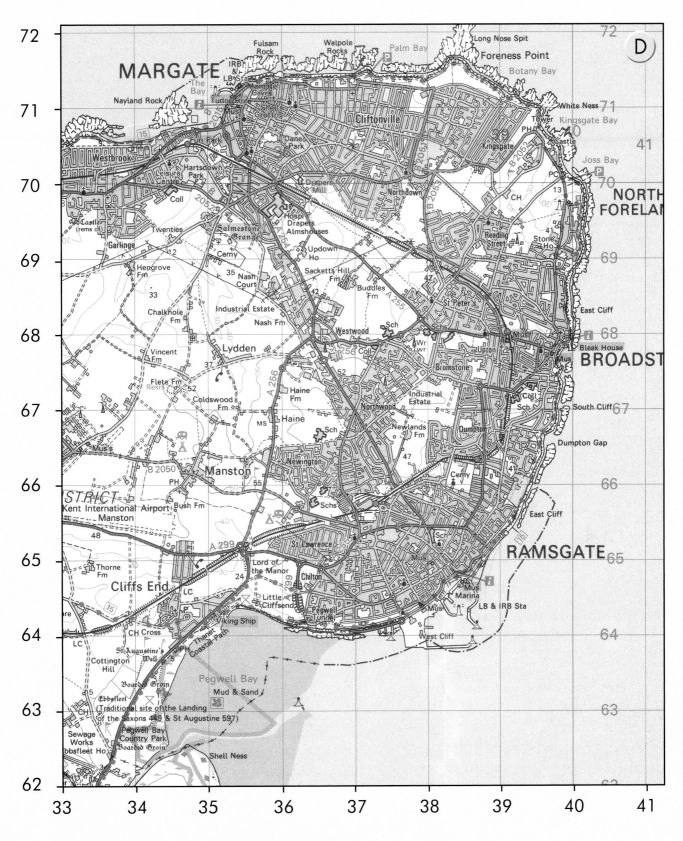

▲ An O.S. map of part of East Kent (with a scale of 1:50,000).

Use your skills: Finding features

You now know that contour patterns tell us a lot
about the landscape of an area. Look at the following
contour map and illustrations to test your knowledge.
You can refer back to pages 16-17 and 20-21 if you
need some reminders!

1 The map below shows contour patterns as well as
   other features such as a road, a river, a lake, a church
   and a settlement. Can you name the six different kinds
   of relief illustrated by the contour patterns A - F?

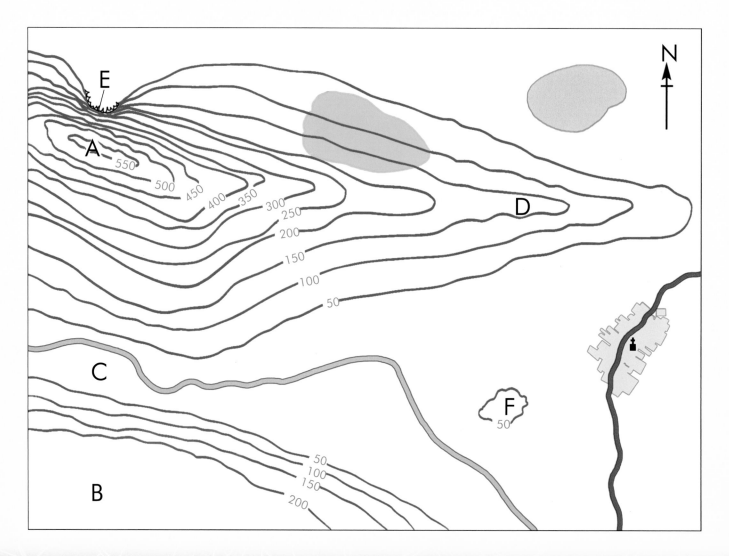

2 The two landscapes in Figures A and B show
different views of the area on the contour map.
Which compass directions are they taken from?

3 Now explain why you made these two decisions!
Do this by referring to the human and natural
features in each landscape.

Use your skills: Crossword

Make a photocopy of this page and use the clues to complete the crossword. The letters down the middle should give the name of a company that makes maps of the whole of the UK.

1 Symbol which gives the exact height at one place on a map.

2 The steepness of a slope.

3 A long, narrow area of high land.

4 Line joining places which are at the same height above sea level.

5 Map stored in the mind?

6 Where a place is.

7 Very steep rock-face.

8 The height and shape of the land.

9 How easy a place is to get to.

10 Mountains, rivers and roads are all examples of these.

11 A map-maker.

12 Long strip of lowland between two areas of much higher land, with a river at the bottom.

13 Flat-topped hill or mountain.

14 Drawing, letter or shading which shows a kind of feature on a map.

Glossary

Aerial photograph   A photograph taken from above the ground. Aerial photographs can be vertical (straight downwards) or oblique (downwards, but at an angle).

Bird's eye view   A view of the Earth's surface as seen from just above it.

By-pass   A modern road built around part of a town or city.

Cartographer   Someone who draws maps.

Central Business District (C.B.D.)   The central area of a town or city, where most of its shops and offices are located.

Contour   A line that joins places that are at exactly the same height above sea level.

Co-ordinates   Letters and numbers that help you to find things on a map grid.

Direction   The way a person or feature is pointing towards something else (given as a compass direction or a bearing).

Feature   A part of a landscape, such as a house or a wood.

Field sketch   A drawing of a landscape that is labelled to show its most important features.

Gradient   Describing how steep a slope is.

Grid reference   A group of numbers used to locate a place on a map.

Human landscape   All the features, such as roads and buildings, that people have added to a natural landscape.

Location   Used to describe where a place is.

Mental map   The image of a map stored in someone's memory.

Ordnance Survey (O.S.)   A company that produces sets of maps at different scales covering the whole of the United Kingdom.

Relief   The height and shape of the land.

Ring road   A modern road built around a town or city so that passing traffic doesn't have to drive through its built-up area.

Scale   A way of showing how much smaller a map is than its real, life-size area. This can be shown in three ways: line scale, ratio scale and statement of scale.

Settlements   Places where people live, such as villages, towns and cities. Linear settlements are long and narrow. Nucleated settlements have a more rounded shape.

Sketch map   A hand-drawn map that is labelled to show its most important features.

Spot height   The height of a place above sea level. Maps often show the spot heights of hilltops and places along roads.

Street map   A map that shows streets and their names. Street maps usually have a number-letter grid.

Symbol   A small letter or drawing showing one kind of map feature.

Thematic map   A map that shows just one type of information.

Topographical map   A map that shows both the physical and the human features of an area.

Index and answers

Answers

p5 1a) The walls and windows of buildings. **1b)** The names of streets, colleges and other buildings; different colours to show buildings, lawns and roads. **1c)** What the buildings and their roofs are made of and what they actually look like. **p6 1a)** Huddersfield Library C2; Huddersfield Railway Station B4 **1b)** A3 **1c)** B2 **1d)** D2 **2a)** Buses **2b)** Cloth **2c)** Viaduct **2d)** It becomes part of the Huddersfield ring road **p12 1a)** False **1b)** True **1c)** True **1d)** True **2)** Belgium – Zeebrugge; Denmark – Esbjerg; England – Dover, Harwich, Hull, Newcastle; France – Dunkirk; Germany – Hamburg; Netherlands – Rotterdam; Norway – Bergen, Stavanger; Scotland – Aberdeen. **p14 1a)** 9420 **1b)** 9323 **1c)** 9529 **1d)** 9422 **2a)** Black Hill **2b)** Little Law **2c)** Hawkwood Hill **2d)** Coupland Hill **3)** Building; Contour; Main road; Motorway; Other road/drive/track; River; Spot height **p17 1)** South; West; North-west; North; 4.2; 3.6; 2.5; 5.9; East/right. **p21 1)** c **2)** d **3)** f **4)** a **5)** b **6)** e **p26 1a)** A Drapers Mill (a windmill); B Viking ship; C The Marina at Ramsgate **1b)** A 363 700 / 363 701; B 352 643; C 385 645 **2a)** approx 3 km; approx 3.5 km **2b)** North-east. **3a)** There is a road between the golf course and the club house. **3b) Activities:** e.g. Camping; Caravanning; Golf; Picnicking. **Places/things to visit:** e.g. Marina; Museums; Public houses (pubs); Ramsgate's Information Centre. **3c)** 683 693 has curved streets and cul-de-sacs. 390 705 has straight, parallel streets. The old, terraced houses in 390 705 were built first. **3d)** e.g. museums, churches, college, railway station. **3e)** Linear, because the buildings are beside the long, narrow road. **p28 a)** A mountain (or hill) top; B plateau or flat-topped mountain; C valley; D ridge; E cliff; F knoll. **p29 b)** A North; B East **c)** A – because the lake is in front of the village and the wood is to the left of the steep cliff. B – because the lake is to the right of the village and the river valley is behind the village. **p30 1** Spot height, **2** Gradient **3** Ridge **4** Contour **5** Mental **6** Location **7** Cliff **8** Relief **9** Access **10** Features **11** Cartographer **12** Valley **13** Plateau **14** Symbol. The company name is Ordnance Survey.